Samuel Parker

A Sermon

Preached before His Honor the Lieutenant-Governor

Samuel Parker

A Sermon
Preached before His Honor the Lieutenant-Governor

ISBN/EAN: 9783337173654

Printed in Europe, USA, Canada, Australia, Japan

Cover: Foto ©Suzi / pixelio.de

More available books at **www.hansebooks.com**

Dr. *PARKER*'s

ELECTION SERMON.

MAY 29, 1793.

COMMONWEALTH OF MASSACHUSETTS.

IN SENATE, May 29, 1793.

ORDERED, That THOMAS DAWES, and BENJAMIN AUSTIN, jun. Efquires, be a Committee to wait on the Rev. Doctor SAMUEL PARKER, and thank him in the name of the SENATE, for the SERMON delivered by him this day, before his Honor the LIEUTENANT-GOVERNOR, the Honorable COUNCIL, and the two Branches of the LEGISLATURE; and to requeft of him a Copy thereof for the Prefs.

Atteft.

SAMUEL COOPER, Clerk.

A

SERMON,

PREACHED BEFORE

His Honor the Lieutenant-Governor,

THE

HONORABLE THE COUNCIL,

AND THE

HONORABLE THE SENATE,

AND

HOUSE OF REPRESENTATIVES,

OF THE

COMMONWEALTH

OF

MASSACHUSETTS,

MAY 29, 1793;

BEING THE DAY OF

GENERAL ELECTION.

BY SAMUEL PARKER, D. D.

RECTOR OF *TRINITY CHURCH*, BOSTON.

PRINTED AT BOSTON,
BY Thomas Adams, PRINTER TO THE HONORABLE GENERAL COURT.
M,DCC,XCIII.

A N

ELECTION SERMON.

PROVERBS xiv. 34.

*RIGHTEOUSNESS EXALTETH A NATION : BUT SIN IS A RE-
PROACH TO ANY PEOPLE.*

T H E great fource of all human know-
ledge is experience ; and that experience which teaches
us practical wifdom, and informs us of the many evils
that conftantly wait on life, is acquired chiefly by obfervation and reflection. Time, indeed, is continu-
ally forcing the inftructions of this fage monitor on
our notice, and when " length of days" has not made
us fufficiently acquainted with her, we fly to the aged
that we may learn her counfels ; or read them with
fufficient certainty, in the mifconduct, difappoint-
ment, and miferies of others.

THE Hiftorian makes it his peculiar glory, that by
faithfully recording the fates of kingdoms, by delinea-
ting the virtues which raifed fome to magnificence,
and

and the vices which brought others gradually to deftruction, he anticipates·the future by a true reprefentation of the paft, and teaches men wifdom by'the example of others. But though, from the fhort period of human life, the narrownefs of our views, and the neceffary calls of duty, we are obliged to recur to the experience of thofe who have gone before us, for almoft all our knowledge; yet the few events that happen to ourfelves, or that fall within the circle of our own obfervation, make a far more lafting impreffion on us, and have a much greater influence over the heart,

THE ftrange viciffitudes of fortune, that happen either to nations or individuals, we hear with faint emotion, and often regard them only as they ferve to gratify curiofity, and increafe our ftore of knowledge. The Hiftorian's eloquence, and the Poet's fancy can fcarcely raife the tear of fympathy, while they relate, with all the decoration of language, the miferies of life; and thofe forrows which only the beft and fofteft bofoms feel occafionally for the calamities of others, are but of fhort duration. They vanifh quick as the morning dews diffolve before the rifing fun, and oft, like them, "leave not a trace behind." But fuch calamities and difappointments as befal ourfelves, are confidered as dear bought experience, and treafured up in the heart. Thefe are the counfellors that will make us wife and good; unlefs in defpite of reafon and of nature, we fuffer life to glide away unnoticed, without improvement in knowledge or in virtue.

SERIOUS

SERIOUS reflection on what has paffed, with a con-ſtant habit of comparing it to the future, ſeems, in-deed, to be a rule of moral diſcipline, natural to the mind of man, and is one of the greateſt ſafeguards of virtue, as well as the beſt means of acquiring uſeful knowledge. The fluctuating ſtate of our minds makes it neceſſary to take theſe retroſpective views of life, that we may increaſe in prudence, and eſtabliſh our-ſelves in virtue.

UNDER the full perſuaſion of the efficacy of this principle, as well as the influence of the Divine Spirit, the Proverbs of Solomon, which have always been eſteemed a moſt valuable part of the holy Scriptures, were written. He ſays himſelf, that they were the fruits of his moſt profound meditations, and of his moſt excellent wiſdom. Becauſe the Preacher was wiſe, he ſtill taught the people knowledge; yea he gave good heed, and ſought out, and ſet in order many Proverbs.* To give the more weight and dig-nity to his precepts, he delivers them not as his own, but as thoſe of Wiſdom herſelf; and in the poetic and dramatic way, introduces her as a divine perſon, the favourite offspring and firſt born of God, who dwelt with him before the foundations of the earth were laid, before time and the world was, and who is ſent forth from him to guide, and inſtruct the children of men.

AMONG theſe Proverbs or wiſe ſayings, we find many excellent rules for the conduct of human life, and for leading men to happineſs. But perhaps there is not any thing in the whole book, of greater im-portance

* Ecclef. xii. 9.

portance to us, as members of civil fociety, than the aphorifm contained in our text. Righteoufnefs exalteth a nation, but fin is a reproach to any people.

It is well known, that the word *righteoufnefs* is ufed, in the facred writings, with different degrees of latitude. Sometimes, it is applied in a confined fenfe, as fignifying that uprightnefs, equity and juftice, which we fhould maintain in our treatment of our fellow creatures, by rendering to all their proper dues; and is fynonimous with juftice. But the word is ufually taken in a more extenfive fignification, as defcriptive of goodnefs in general. In this fenfe the righteous man is one, who acts well in all the relations and characters in which he is placed; who lives in the practice of piety, benevolence, felf government and univerfal goodnefs. In this larger meaning, the term is moft commonly ufed throughout the Pfalms, the Proverbs and the New Teftament. Thus, To him that foweth righteoufnefs fhall be a fure reward. As righteoufnefs tendeth to life, fo he that purfueth evil, purfueth it to his own death. It is in this extenfive fenfe, that the word is undoubtedly ufed in our text. A righteous perfon is one who maintains an upright, holy and virtuous part through the whole courfe and tenor of his life. He is one, who ferioufly confiders, and fteadily difcharges the general obligations of piety and goodnefs. This, no doubt, will neceffarily include in it, his being righteous in the ftrict and limited fignification of the term. He makes a point of preferving an exact fidelity and equity in his intercourfe with mankind. According to the beft of his

abilities

abilities he renders to his fellow creatures their dues, and treats them in a manner agreeable to the various claims, of one kind and another, which they have upon him. He is true to his engagements, and faithful to his promiſes.

BESIDES this, he performs the other offices and duties of the virtuous character. He is not only honeſt and equitable, but kind and benevolent. He endeavours to promote the welfare of thoſe around him, and to behave, in every reſpect, as one who is animated with the principles of affection to his brethren of the human nature. He makes it his labour, his delight, to render them happy, ſo far as the capacity of doing it, which Providence hath put in his power, extends.

NOR, while he is juſt and generous towards men, is he unjuſt to, or forgetful of, the ever bleſſed GOD. He ſeriouſly conſiders his obligations to the greateſt and beſt of beings, and is ſolicitous to teſtify his ſenſe of them, by all the returns which he is capable of making. Hence he cultivates the deepeſt reverence for the ſacred name of his Maker, and the warmeſt ſentiments of devotion towards him. Hence he loves his high Creator and Benefactor, above every object beſide, is truly thankful for the mercies he receives from him, truſts in his protection and ſupport, ſubmits to his will, and is obedient to his commands.

EQUALLY intent is the righteous man upon maintaining and cheriſhing the perſonal virtues. He keeps

B

himſelf

himfelf in the exercife of felf government, temperance, moderation, meeknefs, humility and contentment. In fhort, he endeavours to be found in all the commandments and ordinances of the Lord blamelefs, and to preferve all the graces of the fpiritual life.

Such is the righteoufnefs the wife man fpeaks of as exhibited in practice ; and a righteous nation confifts of a number of individuals whofe character and conduct are fuch as we have now briefly delineated.

The fin mentioned in our text, as the reproach of a people, muft be confidered as the oppofite to this great and good character. When the people compofing a nation fhew no regard to the eternal rules of equity and juftice ; when true religion decays, and they lofe their reverence for the Divine Being ; when they defpife his inftitutions, and profane his fabbaths ; when they ridicule his word, and indulge themfelves in the breach of his commands ; when infidelity and vice prevail ; when impiety and irreligion mark the character of a people—then iniquity abounds, and they are under the influence of that fin, which is their greateft reproach.

Taking then the word righteoufnefs in the fenfe we have explained it, to fignify religion and virtue in general, our text naturally prefents us with a fubject, which, I flatter myfelf, will not be confidered as altogether foreign from the defign of our prefent affembling, viz. THE HARMONY OF RELIGION AND CIVIL POLITY;

ᴛʏ ; or, that religion and virtue are the fureſt means of promoting national happineſs and proſperity.

Wʜᴇɴ Solomon aſſerts that religion or righteouſ- neſs exalteth a nation, we are not to underſtand the propoſition in ſo ſtrict and abſolute a ſenſe, as that true religion is ſo neceſſary, *in all its doctrines*, and in all the extent of its precepts, that there have been no in- ſtances of the proſperity of ſocieties, which have not been wholly regulated by it. Some States, it muſt be acknowledged, which have been only partially govern- ed by its maxims, have enjoyed long and glorious ad- vantages upon the theatre of the world ; either becauſe their falſe religions contained ſome principles of recti- tude, in common with the true religion ; or, becauſe Goᴅ, in order to animate and encourage ſuch people to the practice of ſome virtues, neceſſary to the very being of ſociety, annexed ſucceſs to the exerciſe of them ; or, becauſe rectitude was never ſo fully eſtab- liſhed upon earth, as to preclude injuſtice from en- joying the advantages of virtue, or virtue from ſuffer- ing the penalties of vice. However this may be, we affirm, that the moſt ſure method that a nation can take to ſupport and exalt itſelf, is to follow the laws of righteouſneſs, and the ſpirit of religion.

Nᴏʀ is it aſſerted in our text, that, in *every par- ticular caſe*, religion is more ſucceſsful in procuring ſome temporary advantage than the violation of it ; ſo that to conſider ſociety only in this point of light, and to confine it to this particular caſe, independent- ly of all other circumſtances, religion yields the ho- nour

nour of temporary profperity to injuftice. Some State crimes may have been fuccefsful, and have been the fteps by which certain nations have acquired worldly glory. And fhould we acknowledge that virtue has fometimes been an obftacle to grandeur, ftill the truth of the propofition in our text ftands unimpeached—that if we confider a nation in every point of light, and in all circumftances, it will be found that the more a fociety practifes virtue, the more profperity it will enjoy ; the more it abandons itfelf to vice, the more mifery it will fooner or later fuffer ; fo that the very vice which contributed to its exaltation, will produce its deftruction, and the virtue which feemed at firft to abafe it, will in the end exalt its glory.

WE obferve further here, that by a nation's being exalted, the infpired author of our text does not intend fuch an elevation as worldly heroes, or rather tyrants, aim at. If, by exalting a nation, is underftood an elevation extending itfelf beyond the limits of rectitude ; an elevation not directed by juftice and good faith, confifting in the acquifitions of wanton and arbitrary power, obliging other nations to fubmit to a yoke of flavery, and thus becoming an executioner of divine vengeance on all mankind—we allow, that in this fenfe, exaltation is not an effect of righteoufnefs. But, by exalting a nation, the wife man intends, whatever promotes the greateft happinefs and profperity of its citizens ; its being governed by wife and wholefome laws, enjoying liberty and equal government, negociating fuccefsful treaties, attacking its enemies with courage, defending itfelf with refolution,

enjoying

enjoying every blefling conducive to the profperity and happinefs of a people ; and at the fame time blefled with the favourable notice and regard of the Divine Being. Such an exaltation is obtained only by righteoufnefs.

In a word, it is not the lot of humanity, that the profperity of any nation fhould be fo perfect, as to exclude all untoward circumftances. The meaning of our text muft be, that the higheft glory, and the moft perfect happinefs, which can be enjoyed by a nation, in a world, where, after all, there muft be a mixture of adverfity with profperity, are the fruits of righteoufnefs. No nation was ever yet free from evils and inconveniences of many kinds ; and even the moft virtuous focieties have been fuffered to labour under many ftraits and difficulties ; and it muft be allowed, that this world will always be to publick bodies what it is to individuals, a place of mifery and unhappinefs ; and therefore we muft underftand our text as afferting only, that the moft folid happinefs, which can be enjoyed here below, has righteoufnefs for its caufe. It is the more neceffary to reftrain it within thefe limitations, not only becaufe they explain the fenfe of the infpired author, but becaufe they ferve to preclude fuch objections, to unravel fuch fophifms, and to folve fuch difficulties, as infidels and libertines have urged againft its truth.

To prove, then, that religion and virtue are the fureft means of promoting national happinefs and profperity, let us confider the origin of civil government, and the motives which induced mankind to

unite

unite themſelves in ſociety. By doing this, we ſhall perceive that righteouſneſs is the only thing that can render nations happy.

EVERY individual has a great variety of wants, and but few, and thoſe very limited, faculties to ſupply them. Every individual of mankind has need of knowledge to inform him, of laws to direct him, of property to ſupport him, of food to nouriſh him, of clothing and covering to defend him againſt the in‑clemencies of the ſeaſons. This catalogue of our va‑rious and reſpective wants might eaſily be enlarged. Similar intereſts form a ſimilar deſign. Divers men unite themſelves together, in order that the induſtry of all may ſupply the wants of each. Hence the origin of ſocieties and publick bodies of men.

THE Author of our being has alſo given to man a nature fitted for, and diſpoſed to, ſociety. It was not good for man at firſt to be alone; his nature is ſocial, having various affections, propenſities and paſ‑ſions, which reſpect ſociety, and cannot be indulged without a ſocial intercourſe. The natural principles of benevolence, compaſſion, juſtice, and indeed moſt of our natural affections, powerfully incite to, and plainly indicate that man was formed for, ſociety.

THE ſocial affections of our nature, and the deſire of the many conveniences, not to be obtained or en‑joyed, without the concurrence of others, probably firſt induced men to aſſociate together. But the de‑pravity of our nature ſince the apoſtacy, and the great

prevalency

prevalency of lufts and corruptions, have obliged mankind to enter into clofer connexions and combina-
tions, for mutual protection and affiftance. Thus
civil focieties and governments were formed, and in
this way government comes from God, and is his or-
dinance. The kingdom is the Lord's, and he is the
Governor among the nations. By him kings reign,
and princes decree juftice, even all the judges of the
earth.

THE end and defign of civil fociety and government, from this view of its origin, muft be to fecure
the rights and properties of its members, and to promote their welfare and happinefs ; or, in the words of
infpiration, that men may live quiet and peaceable
lives, in all godlinefs and honefty.

IT is eafy to perceive then, that in order to enjoy the
bleffings propofed by this affemblage, fome fixed maxims muft be laid down, and inviolably obeyed. It is
neceffary that all the members of this body fhould
confider themfelves as naturally equal ; that by this
idea they may be inclined to afford each other mutual
fuccour. It is requifite that they fhould be fincere to
each other, left deceit fhould ferve for a veil to con-
ceal the finifter defigns of fome from the eyes of the
reft. The rigid rules of equity fhould be inviolably
obferved, that fo they may fulfil the contracts, which
they bound themfelves to perform, when they were
admitted into this fociety. Efteem and benevolence
ought to give life and action to righteoufnefs. It is
of the utmoft confequence, that the happinefs of all
                                                 fhould

fhould be preferred before the intereft of an individual; and that in cafes where publick and private interefts clafh, the publick good fhould always prevail. Every citizen ought to cultivate his own talents, that he may contribute to the happinefs of that fociety, to which he ought to devote himfelf with the utmoft fincerity and zeal. Thefe duties are abfolutely neceffary for the welfare and profperity of focieties. And what can be more proper to make us obferve thefe rules than religion,—than righteoufnefs? Religion brings us to feel our natural equality; it teaches us that we originate in the fame duft; have the fame GOD for our Creator; are all defcended from the fame firft Parent; all partake of the fame miferies, and are all doomed to the fame laft end. Religion teaches us fincerity to each other; that the tongue fhould be a faithful interpreter of the mind; that we fhould fpeak every man truth with his neighbour; and, that being always in the fight of the GOD of truth, we fhould never deviate from the laws of truth. Religion teaches us that we fhould be juft; that we fhould render to all their dues; tribute to whom tribute is due; cuftom to whom cuftom; fear to whom fear; honour to whom honour; that whatfoever we would men fhould do unto us, we fhould do even fo unto them. Religion requires us to be animated with charity,— to confider each other as creatures of one GOD, fubjects of the fame heavenly King, members of one body, and heirs of the fame glory. It requires us to give up our private intereft to the publick good, not to feek our own, but every one another's wealth; it even requires us to lay down our lives for the brethren.

Thus

Thus if we confider nations in thefe primitive views, it is righteoufnefs alone that exalts them.

WERE we to defcend from thefe general principles, and take into view the particular forms of government, which have been adopted by the various nations upon earth; or rather, which have grown out of particular occafions and emergencies; from the fluctuating policy of different ages; from the contentions, fuccefses, interefts and opportunities of different orders and parties of men among them (for fuch we fhall find was the origin of moft of the particular forms of government in the world,) we fhall be convinced that each nation has been, more or lefs happy, in its own mode of governing, has more or lefs prevented the inconveniences, to which its form of government is fubject, according as it has been more or lefs attached to religion or righteoufnefs. The precepts and the maxims of religion, applied to thefe imperfections, would effectually reftrain all thofe excefses, and preclude thofe evils, from which the moft perfect forms of government are not entirely free. But the time will not permit us to enter into fo particular an inquiry, or to multiply quotations to prove this point.

I PROCEED to obferve, fecondly, that the doctrine of Providence will furnifh us with another argument, to prove the truth of our text.

THE conduct of Providence, with regard to publick bodies is very different from that, which prevails in the cafe of individuals. It is a rule in the divine government,

ment, to deal with nations according to their moral
character. Perfect juſtice is the invariable rule of his
dominion over publick bodies. In regard to individuals, Providence is involved in darkneſs. Many times
it ſeems to condemn virtue, and crown injuſtice ; to
leave innocence to groan in ſilence, and to empower
guilt to riot, and triumph in publick. The wicked
rich man fared ſumptuouſly every day, while Lazarus
deſired, in vain, to be fed with the crumbs that fell
from his table. St. Paul was executed on a ſcaf-
fold, while Nero reigned on Cæſar's throne.

But Providence is directed in a different method,
in regard to publick bodies. Proſperity in them is
the effect of righteouſneſs ; publick happineſs is the
reward of publick virtue ; the wiſeſt nation is uſually
the moſt ſucceſsful, and "virtue walks with glory by
"her ſide." The work of righteouſneſs ſhall be
peace, and the effects of righteouſneſs, quietneſs and
aſſurance forever. On the other hand, the judgments
of Heaven are commonly ſhowered down upon a
wicked people ; he turneth a fruitful land into bar-
renneſs, for the wickedneſs of them that dwell therein.

God ſometimes, indeed, afflicts the moſt virtuous
nations ; but he does ſo with the deſign of purifying
them, and of opening new occaſions to beſtow larger
benefits upon them. He ſometimes, indeed, proſpers
wicked nations ; but their proſperity is an effort of
his patience and long ſuffering ; it is to give them
time to prevent their deſtruction, and by his goodneſs,
to lead them to repentance. But, as before obſerved,

proſperity

profperity *ufually* follows, righteoufnefs in publick bodies; publick happinefs is the reward of publick virtue; the wifeft nation is the moft fuccefsful, and glory is *generally* connected with virtue. And this conduct of Providence is grounded on this reafon. A day will come when Lazarus will be indemnified, and the rich man punifhed; when St. Paul will be rewarded, and Nero will be confounded. Innocence will be avenged, juftice fatisfied, the majefty of the laws repaired, and the rights of God maintained.

But fuch a retribution is impracticable in regard to publick bodies. A nation cannot then be punifhed as a nation, nor a kingdom as a kingdom. All the different forms of government will then be abolifhed. While fome of the human race are put into poffeffion of glory, others will be covered with fhame and confufion of face. It feems then, that Providence owes to its own rectitude, thofe times of vengeance, in which it pours all its wrath on wicked nations; fends them wars, famines, plagues and other cataftrophes, of which, hiftory gives us fo many memorable examples. To place hopes altogether on worldly policy; to pretend to derive advantages from vice, and fo to found the happinefs of fociety, on the ruins of religion and virtue, is little fhort of infulting Providence. It is to aroufe that power againft us, which, fooner or later, overwhelms and confounds vicious focieties.

But if the obfcurity of the ways of Providence, which ufually renders doubtful, our reafonings upon the divine conduct, weaken this argument, let us confider the declarations of God himfelf upon this point.

The

THE whole 28th chapter of Deuteronomy, all the blessings and curses pronounced there, fully prove our doctrine. Read the tender complaint, which GOD formerly made concerning the irregularities of his people. O that they were wife, that they understood this, that they would consider their latter end ! How should one chafe a thousand, and two put ten thousand to flight. Agreeably to this, are the affecting words uttered by the mouth of the Psalmist—O that my people had hearkened unto me, and Israel had walked in my ways. I should soon have subdued their enemies, and turned mine hand against their adversaries. Their time should have endured forever. I should have fed them also, with the fineft of the wheat, and with honey out of the rock should I have satisfied them. What noble promises are made also by the ministry of Isaiah ? Thus faith the Lord thy Redeemer, the Holy One of Israel, I am the Lord thy God which teacheth thee to profit ; which leadeth thee by the way thou shouldft go. O that thou hadft hearkened to my commandments ! then had thy peace been as a river, and thy righteoufnefs as the waves of the sea ; thy feed also had been as the sand, and thy name should not have been cut off, nor deftroyed before me. Observe also the terrible threatnings, denounced against backfliding Israel, by the prophet Jeremiah. Though Mofes and Samuel ftood before me, yet my mind could not be toward this people ; caft them out of my fight, and let them go forth. And it shall come to pafs, if they fay unto thee, Whither shall we go forth ? Then thou shalt tell them ; Thus faith the Lord, Such as are for death to death, and fuch as are for the fword to

the

the fword, and fuch as are for the famine to the famine, and fuch as are for captivity to captivity. Thou haſt forſaken me, ſaith the Lord, thou art gone backward ; therefore will I ſtretch out my hand againſt thee, and deſtroy thee : I am weary of repenting.

Not to multiply quotations ; we find that through the whole hiſtory of the Old Teſtament, the inter-changeable providences of God, towards the Jewiſh nation, were always ſuited to their manners. They were conſtantly proſperous or afflicted, according as religion and righteouſneſs flouriſhed, or declined among them.

Nor was this Providence exerciſed only towards his own people, but he dealt thus with other nations, as their hiſtory evinces ; and thus the truth of our text is proved by experience. Were we to conſult the ancient hiſtory of the Egyptians, the Perſians, or the Romans, who ſurpaſſed them all, we ſhall find they were by turns exalted, as they reſpected righteouſneſs, or abaſed, as they neglected it.

By what myſterious art did ancient Egypt ſubſiſt, with ſo much glory, during the period of fifteen or ſix-teen ages.* By a benevolence ſo extenſive, that he, who refuſed to relieve the wretched, when he had it in his power to aſſiſt him, was himſelf puniſhed with death : by a juſtice ſo impartial, that their kings obliged the judges to take an oath, that they would adminiſter impartial juſtice to all, though they, the kings themſelves, ſhould command the contrary : by

an

* Diodor. Siculus. Herodotus lib. 2.

an averfion to bad princes fo fixed, as to deny them
the honours of a funeral : by entertaining fuch juft
ideas of the vanity of life, as to confider their houfes
as inns, in which they were to lodge, as it were, only
for a night ; and their fepulchres as habitations in
which they were to abide for many ages ; for which
reafon, they united, in their famous pyramids, all the
folidity and pomp of architecture : by a life fo labo-
rious, that even their amufements were adapted to
ftrengthen the body, and improve the mind : by fuch
a remarkable readinefs to difcharge their debts, that
they had a law, which prohibited the borrowing of
money, except on condition of pledging the body of
a parent for payment ; a depofit fo venerable, that a
man who deferred the redemption of it, was looked
upon with horror : in a word, by a wifdom fo profound, that Mofes himfelf is renowned in Scripture for
being learned in it.

THE Perfians, alfo, obtained a diftinguifhed place
of honour, in ancient hiftory, by confidering falfehood
in the moft odious light ; as a vice the meaneft and
moft difgraceful ; by a noble generofity, conferring
favours on the nations they had conquered, and feav-
ing them to enjoy all the enfigns of their former grandeur ; by an univerfal equity, obliging themfelves to
publifh the virtues of their greateft enemies ; by edu-
cating their children fo wifely, that they were taught
virtue, as other nations were taught letters. The
children of the royal family, and of the nobles, were,
at an early period of life, put under the tuition of
four of the wifeft and moft virtuous ftatefmen. The

firft

firſt taught them the worſhip of the gods; the
ſecond trained them up to ſpeak truth, and practice
equity; the third habituated them to ſubdue volup-
tuouſneſs, and to enjoy real liberty; to be always
maſters of themſelves and of their own paſſions; and
the fourth inſpired them with courage; and by teach-
ing them how to command themſelves, taught them
how to rule over others.

* The Romans founded their ſyſtem of policy upon
that beſt and wiſeſt principle, the fear of the gods; a
firm belief of a divine ſuperintending Providence, and
a future ſtate of rewards and puniſhments. Their
children were trained up in this belief from tender in-
fancy, which took root and grew up with them, by
the influence of an excellent education, where they
had the benefit of example, as well as precept.
Hence we read of no heathen nation in the world,
where both the publick and private duties of religion,
were ſo ſtrictly adhered to, and ſo ſcrupulouſly obſerved, as among the Romans. They imputed their
good or bad ſucceſs to the obſervance of theſe duties,
and they received publick proſperity, or publick calamities, as bleſſings conferred, or puniſhments in-
flicted, by their gods. Though the ceremonies of
their religion juſtly appear to us, inſtances of the moſt
abſurd and moſt extravagant ſuperſtition, yet, as they
were eſteemed the moſt eſſential acts of religion, by the
Romans, they muſt conſequently carry all the force
of a religious principle. † Cicero, the great Roman
orator and philoſopher, ſpeaking of his countrymen,
says,

---

* Montague's Letters.
† Cicero de Harus. Reſp. p. 183.

says, We neither exceeded the Spaniards in number, nor did we excel the Gauls in strength of body, nor the Carthagenians in craft, nor the Greeks in arts and sciences: But we have indisputably surpassed all the nations in the universe, in piety and attachment to religion, and in the only point that can be called true wisdom, a thorough conviction, that all things here below, are directed and governed by Divine Providence. To this principle alone, he wisely attributes the grandeur and good fortune of his country. From this principle proceeded that respect for, and submission to, their laws; and that temperance, moderation, and contempt for wealth, which are the best defence against the encroachments of injustice and oppression. Hence too arose that inextinguishable love for their country, which, next to the gods, they looked upon as the chief object of veneration. * This they carried to such an height of enthusiasm, as to make every tie of social love, natural affection, and self preservation, give way to this duty to their dearer country. Hence proceeded that obstinate and undaunted courage, that insuperable contempt of danger, and death itself, in defence of their country, which complete the idea of the Roman character, as it is drawn by the historians, in the virtuous ages of the republick. As long as the manners of the Romans were regulated by this first great principle of religion, they were free and invincible. But the atheistical doctrine of Epicurus, which insinuated itself at Rome, under the respectable name of Philosophy, undermined and destroyed this ruling principle. The luxuries of the East, after the conquest conqueft of Afia, corrupted the manners of the Romans, weakened this principle of religion, and prepared them for the reception of atheifm, which is the never failing attendant on luxury. And thus, by their rapid and unexampled degeneracy, was brought on the total fubverfion of that mighty republick.

WERE we to inquire into the reafons of their decline; were we to compare the Egyptians under their wife kings, with the Egyptians in a time of anarchy; the Perfians victorious under Cyrus, with the Perfians enervated by the luxuries of Afia; the Romans at liberty under their confuls, with the Romans enflaved by their emperors, we fhould find, that the decline of each was owing to fin, which is a reproach to a people; to the practice of vices, oppofite to the virtues which had caufed their elevation; we fhould be obliged to acknowledge, that a total difregard to religion and righteoufnefs; luxury, voluptuoufnefs, difunion, corruption, and boundlefs ambition, were the odious means of fubverting ftates, which, in the heighth of their profperity, expected to endure to the end of time.

HAVING thus eftablifhed the truth contained in our text, let us employ a few moments in reflecting on what has been faid.

IN the firft place. What gratitude is due from us to the King of kings, for affording us better means of knowing the righteoufnefs, that exalts a people, and more motives to practife it, than all the nations of antiquity. They had only a fuperficial, debafed, confufed

D

fufed knowledge of the virtues, which conftitute fub-
ftantial grandeur; and as they held errors in religion,
they muft neceffarily have erred in civil polity. Our
heavenly Father, glory be to his name, has placed at
the head of our councils, the moft perfect Legiflator,
that ever held the reins of government in the world.
This Legiflator is Jefus Chrift. His kingdom, indeed, is not of this world, but the rules, he has given
us to arrive at his heavenly kingdom, are the moft
proper to render us happy in the prefent ftate. When
he fays, Seek ye firft the kingdom of Gop, and his
righteoufnefs, and all other things fhall be added to
you; he gives the command, and makes the promife,
to whole nations, as well as individuals.

Who ever carried, fo far as this divine Legiflator,
ideas of the virtues we have mentioned, and by prac-
tifing which, nations are exalted? Who ever formed
fuch juft notions of that benevolence, that love of focial good, that magnanimity, that generofity to enemies, that wifdom, juftice, and equity, that frugality,
and devotednefs to the publick good, and all the other
virtues, which render antiquity venerable to us?
Who ever gave fuch wife inftructions to kings, and
fubjects; to magiftrates and people; to citizens and
foldiers; to the world and the church? We are better
acquainted with thefe virtues, than moft of the nations in the world. We are able to carry our glory, far beyond the nations of antiquity; if not that
glory, which glares and dazzles, at leaft that which
makes tranquil and happy, and procures a felicity far

preferable

preferable to all the pageantry of heroifm, and worldly fplendor.

Let not thefe things, my friends, be matters of
mere fpeculation to us. Let us endeavour to reduce
them to practice. Never let us fuffer our political
principles to clafh, with the principles of our religion.
Far, far, be from us, and from our rulers, that deceit
and hypocrify, that falfehood and infincerity, that dif-
fimulation and craftinefs, thofe abominable maxims,
which a depraved Florentine * recommended to
ftatefmen. Let us obey the precepts of Jefus Chrift,
and practife that righteoufnefs which exalteth a nation, and by fo doing, we fhall draw down blefﬁngs
on our nation, more pure and perfect than thofe, we
now enjoy. The blefﬁngs we now enjoy, are fuch as
ought, on this aufpicious anniverfary, to infpire us
with lafting gratitude to the great Arbiter of nations,—to him who fetteth up one, and putteth
down another.

It was a favourite method of inftruction with the
Jewifh Legiflators and Prophets, to recur to the hiftory of their nation; to ancient events, and alfo to
fuch as took place, in a period coeval with themfelves,
in order to excite a correfpondent gratitude, and a
fpirit of religious obedience, in the breafts of the people. The time will not admit us to adopt the fame
plan, and enter into fuch an extenfive difcuffion : A
few, however, of the more general, and more confpi-
cuous, you will permit me to glance at.

THE

* Machiavel.

THE firſt is the bleſſing of publick peace. When we look back on the difficulties and dangers, in which the United States were involved, in the late conteſt with Great Britain ; when we reflect on the perils and diſaſters we experienced, when ſurrounded with ſcenes of horror and devaſtation—with the depredations and ſhocking ravages of war—when our liberties, our country, and even life itſelf might be ſaid to " hang in doubt," and contraſt it with the preſent peaceable ſtate of our nation, we muſt acknowledge the gracious interference of almighty GOD, in our favour.

WHILE wars and rumours of wars are now ſpreading, and prevailing through all Europe—while nation is riſing againſt nation, and kingdom againſt kingdom—while the old world is generally convulſed, and tottering under thoſe ſigns and ſymptoms, which denote approaching diſſolution,—to us is given, and as yet continued, the bleſſing of peace.

How long we ſhall enjoy this greateſt of the divine favours, the commotions, which have overſpread the European nations, have rendered very uncertain. No one can doubt, that our intereſt, our ſafety, and our happineſs, as a nation, forbid us to interfere in their quarrels. Whether the faith of treaties, or principles of gratitude, for ſervices performed in our diſtreſs, call upon us to hazard our own peace and proſperity, it is neither prudent, nor proper to diſcuſs, in this place. This is a ſubject that reſts in the Supreme Executive of the United States ; in the wiſdom, firmneſs, and

prudence

prudence of which, we are happy that we can place entire confidence.

THE present appears to be as eventful an æra, as any the annals of mankind can furnish. A combination of events seems to be manifestly tending to bring about some mighty revolution, among the nations of the earth. History has scarcely ever before furnished us, with an instance of a populous, and powerful nation, throwing off the yoke of despotism, and acquiring sentiments and habits, congenial to a great and free republick. We have seen the mists of ignorance and error fast rolling away, and the benign beams of liberty, freedom and science, spreading their lustre over the mighty kingdom of France. The flame caught from America, and the spirit of patriotism illumined that whole nation. What generous mind did not espouse its cause? What friend to liberty, and equal rights did not wish them success?

BUT alas! the fair countenance of freedom has been overspread with a dark veil; and the victims, which popular anarchy and ferocity have sacrificed, must be allowed to have sullied the glories of a revolution, which bid fair to astonish the world. It is, forever to be regretted, that any dark shade of ferocious revenge should eclipse the glory of establishing liberty, and freedom, in that nation. But where do the records of history point out a revolution, unstained by some actions of barbarity? When do the passions of human nature rise to that pitch, which produces great events, without wandering into some irregularities? Perhaps, at so great a distance as we are placed, and with so small means of
authentick

authentick information, we are not capable of form=
ing a proper judgment of their conduct, and the reafons of all their actions; but muſt patiently wait for
the pen of the impartial hiſtorian, to enable us to de-
cide, how far to juſtify or condemn. Should an apolo-
gy, for that mental intoxication that ſeems to have
influenced them, be neceſſary, or proper to be here in-
ferted, permit me to give it, in the words of a very
ſprightly female writer.*   "Let us remember," ſays
ſhe, "that the great cauſe of liberty remains uncon-
" taminated, by the aſſaſſinations at Liſle. Though
" fanatical bigots, in the rage of ſuperſtitious cruelty,
" have dragged their victims to the ſtake, would it be
" rational to extend our abhorrence of ſuch actions
" to Chriſtianity itſelf ?—to that benevolent religion,
" which inculcates univerſal charity, love and good
" will towards men ; and chooſe the comfortleſs, the
" ſullen indifference of atheiſm ? And ſhall we, becauſe
" the fanatics of liberty have committed ſome deteſ-
" table crimes, conclude that liberty is an evil, and
" prefer the gloomy tranquillity of deſpotiſm ? If the
" bleſſings of freedom have ſometimes been abuſed,
" it is becauſe they are not well underſtood. Thoſe
" occaſional evils, which have happened in the infant
" ſtate of liberty, are but the effects of deſpotiſm.
" Men have been long treated with inhumanity, there-
" fore they are ferocious. They have often been be-
" trayed, therefore they are ſuſpicious. They have
" once been ſlaves, and therefore they are tyrants.
" They have been uſed to a ſtate of warfare, and are
" not yet accuſtomed to univerſal benevolence. They
" have

* Helen Maria Williams.

" have long been ignorant, and have not yet attained
" fufficient knowledge. They have been condemned
" to darknefs, and their eyes are dazzled by light.
" The French have thrown afide the ritual of defpot-
" ifm, but they have not all had time to learn the
" liturgy of that new conftitution, which is laid upon
" the altar of their country. But the genuine prin-
" ciples of enlightened freedom will foon be better
" comprehended, and may perhaps, at no diftant pe-
" riod, be adopted by all the nations of Europe. Li-
" berty may bring her fons from afar, and her daugh-
" ters from the ends of the earth.

" THE oppreffions which mankind have fuffered in
" every age, and almoft in every country, will lead
" them to form more perfect fyftems of legiflation, than
" if they had fuffered lefs ; and they will only have to
" regret, that their happinefs has been purchafed, by
" the mifery of paft ages.

" THEN will the reign of humanity, of order, and
" of peace, begin ; the gates of Janus will be forever
" clofed ; liberty will extend her benign influence over
" the nations, and ye fhall know her by her fruits."

BUT to return to ourfelves.

ANOTHER bleffing we enjoy, and which calls aloud
for our gratitude, is the excellent conftitution of our
ftate government, and that of the federal fyftem,
which gives union, order, and happinefs to America.

FEW

FEW nations have ever enjoyed the opportunity, of taking up government upon its firft principles, and of choofing that form, which is adapted to their fituation, and moft productive of their publick interefts and happinefs. "The government of the United "States," fays a political writer,* "approaches neareft "to the focial compact, of any that hiftory can fur- "nifh." Upon an impartial examination of our conftitution of government, we find it the beft calcu- lated for promoting the happinefs, and preferving the lives, liberty, and property of the citizens, of any yet recorded in hiftory. Liberty is here placed in the cuftody of the people. It wifely guards againft anar- chy, and confufion on the one hand, and tyranny, and oppreffion on the other. It is framed upon an extent, not only of civil, but of religious liberty, unexampled, perhaps, in any other country. The facred rights of confcience are fo fecured, that "no citizen can be "hurt, molefted, or reftrained in his perfon, liberty or "eftate, for worfhipping GOD, in the manner and "feafon, moft agreeable to the dictates of his confci- "ence, or for his religious profeffion or fentiments." How fhould this confideration endear it to its citi- zens, and induce them to reverence it—not only calmly to fubmit to it, but to regard it with a vene- ration and affection rifing even to enthufiafm, like that, which prevailed at Sparta, and at Rome.

HAPPY people, whofe lot is fallen to them in plea- fant places, and who have fo goodly an heritage. Hap- py people! if we have wifdom and virtue, to improve aright

* Paley.

aright the advantages we now enjoy. Bleſſed be GOD, who hath viſited, and redeemed his people ; who hath called them to liberty, and granted them the bleſſing of peace, and of a free government.

ONE other favour, you will permit me to mention, is our national proſperity. One bleſſing generally introduces another, and this is the conſequence of peace, and a free government. Our ſwords are now turned into ploughſhares, and our ſpears into pruning hooks. Our ſhips, inſtead of carrying the engines of deſtruction, are now fraught with the ſtores of the merchant, and convey to us, from all quarters of the world, the peculiar treaſures of kings, and the pro-vinces. The riches of the earth, and the abundance of the ſeas, are profuſely poured into our laps.

BUT are we not, by an abuſe of theſe bleſſings, in danger of being deprived of them ? If, having eaten and become full ; having built goodly houſes, and dwelt therein ; and having our ſilver and our gold, and all that we have, greatly multiplied and increaſed ; inſtead of being thankful for theſe bleſſings, and tem-perate in the uſe of them, we become preſumptuouſly lifted up, and forget the Lord our God ; if, while we enjoy the higheſt degree of political liberty and proſ-perity, we are not a virtuous and religious people, ſhall we not provoke the Moſt High to withdraw theſe fa-vours from us, and " to empty us from veſſel to veſ-" ſel ?" If, inſtead of practiſing that righteouſneſs, which exalteth a nation, we indulge a ſpirit of ſelf ex-altation ; what an army of evils will prevail with it ?

E   Luxury

Luxury and excess supersede the enjoyment of the things themselves. Ostentation, in a great measure, supplants the true delights of society, and an emulous superiority in pride, and distinction, contributes materially to the utter annihilation of simple principles, and almost, cuts asunder the cords of genuine, sentimental friendship. The fate of nations confirms a very ancient doctrine of revelation, that whenever publick prosperity causes a forgetfulness of GOD, a contempt of religion, and increasing profligacy, in the manners of a people, that very prosperity shall destroy them.

WITH this declaration, and with the many examples of its truth, recorded in the page of history, let us exert ourselves to perpetuate the great blessings, and privileges we enjoy, by a contrary demeanor, and a more Christian deportment than we have hitherto exercised : for the prolongation of our national charter is entirely dependent thereon ; and the continuance of national prosperity is solely held, by this conditional tenure, the Lord is with us, while we are with him ; if we seek him, he will be found of us, but if we forsake him, he will forsake us.

NOR are we in less danger, from the abuse of our civil liberty, than from that of our prosperity.

CIVIL government is, doubtless, one of the greatest external blessings, of which we are possessed. It is our protection from fraud and injustice—from rapine and violence. It is the security of our lives—of

our

our property—of every thing that is dear to us. The abuſe of liberty is the greateſt of evils, and draws after it, a train of the moſt baneful conſequences. When a people miſimprove their privileges, and become diſorderly, ungovernable, and factious, they introduce a ſtate of anarchy, which is worſe than abſolute deſpotiſm.

No one, of the leaſt reflection, can be inſenſible, what great advantages that nation enjoys, which is not only in a ſtate of perfect peace with its neighbours, but poſſeſſes uninterrupted quiet and tranquillity at home ; which is neither threatened with foreign inſult, nor moleſted by inbred commotions, generally ſpeaking far more dangerous than the former ; at leaſt, when they riſe to any conſiderable heighth. It has, indeed, been ſaid, that "ſmall diſturbances in the ſtate, do the "ſame ſervice that the winds do in the air, by motion "to keep it from ſtagnation and putrefaction :" But when once the winds are raiſed, no one can tell when they will be laid, or how ſtrong they will grow ; and that which was wantonly, or from ſelfiſh views, raiſed, to ſerve a preſent turn, may, in time, come to overturn a conſtitution.

We are not indeed to ſuppoſe, that every ſmall inquietude, every little party or faction, that happens to take place, will be able to accompliſh ſuch extraordinary, ſuch pernicious events ; yet, it will not be diſputed, but that they are liable to produce many fatal, and deſtructive conſequences ; which, though not always immediately apparent, will yet, in time, become
ſufficiently

fufficiently manifeft, by a general corruption of manners, and by breaking loofe from all proper reftraint.

An ingenious writer* juftly obferves, " That a dangerous ambition, oftener lurks behind the fpecious
mafk of zeal for the rights of, the people, than under
the forbidden appearance of enthufiafm, for the firm-
nefs, and efficiency of government. Hiftory will teach
us, that the former, has been found a much more certain road to the introduction of defpotifm, than the
latter ; and that of thofe men who have overturned the
liberty of republicks, the greateft number have begun
their career, by paying an obfequious court to the people, commencing demagogues, and ending tyrants."

How cautious, then, fhould we be, while we are
zealous for liberty, that we do not defpife government,
and weaken the fprings of it, by running into licentiouf-
nefs. A fpirit of faction, of murmuring and dif-
content, may excite internal difcord, which may ac-
complifh that, which external violence was not able to
effect, I mean our independence, liberty, and fafety.

We have no reafon to doubt of the virtues, and
abilities of thofe, whom our own free choice has made
the guardians of our rights, both in the federal and
ftate governments ; we are perfuaded, that their upright and faithful endeavours will be exerted to fecure,
and perpetuate the bleffings of peace, and liberty, and
to promote the true, intereft of this people. While
the meafures of righteoufnefs are religioufly obferved
in

* Federalift.

in their adminiſtrations, we are ſure, they will be crowned with ſucceſs. For it is by righteouſneſs, the throne of government is eſtabliſhed, and the nation is exalted.

We have the happineſs of ſeeing once more, at the head of this Commonwealth, a Gentleman,* of whoſe abilities in the arduous and important ſcience of government—of whoſe patriotiſm and love of liberty— of whoſe integrity and upright intentions we have had long experience. That diſplay of wiſdom, fortitude, and magnanimity, joined with the moſt unremitting attention, and perſeverance, manifeſted in the virtuous ſtruggle, to obtain and ſecure our independence, muſt place his Excellency in the rank of thoſe great and worthy patriots, who have diſtinguiſhed themſelves as the defenders of the rights of mankind : And the many and eminent ſervices he has rendered to this Commonwealth, over which he has ſo often, and ſo long preſided ; as well as his many publick and private virtues, add a luſtre to his character. We ſincerely lament, that the diſcharge of the duties of his high, and important ſtation, is rendered ſo difficult and irkſome, by his Excellency's ill ſtate of health, and the many bodily infirmities with which he has been long afflicted. May the benevolent Parent of the univerſe, who is the health of our countenance, and our God, remove the pains and diſorders, under which his Excellency labours, reſtore and confirm his health, make the remainder of his days happy to himſelf, and uſeful to the Commonwealth, and finally reward all his ſervices with eternal happineſs in his kingdom above.

The

* His Excellency John Hancock, Eſq.

THE patriotiſm, firmneſs, and inflexible attachment to the intereſts of his country, manifeſted by his
Honor, the Lieutenant-Governor,* through a long
ſeries of years, juſtly entitle him to the ſecond rank in
government : And the great unanimity, with which
his Excellency and Honor have, ſo repeatedly, been
elected to their reſpective honourable ſtations, by the
unbiaſſed ſuffrages of their fellow-citizens, is the higheſt atteſtation of their merit. To the gracious protection of almighty GOD we commend them both ;
beſeeching him to grant them wiſdom from above; and
grace to improve their diſtinguiſhed talents, in promoting the true intereſt of this Commonwealth, and
the United States.

THE Gentlemen, who compoſe the two branches of
the General Court, have, many of them, the ſatisfaction
of reflecting, that their former ſervices have proved ac-
ceptable to the multitude of their brethren, by their
being re-elected into the important department of le-
giſlation. In filling up the few vacant ſeats in the Senate, and in chooſing an executive Council, for the en-
ſuing year, which is the firſt object of their concern,
they will not be influenced by perſonal or intereſted
views ; but will elect ſuch out of thoſe, who are the
ſubjects of their choice, as are able men ; ſuch as fear
GOD ; men of truth, hating covetouſneſs.

IT has indeed been doubted by ſome, whether this
rule ſhould, in all caſes, be ſtrictly adhered to ; whether
a man who is not of this deſcription, who is not a man
of rigid probity ; who does not appear to have the fear
of

* His Honor SAMUEL ADAMS, Eſq.

of God before his eyes, and to be governed by a facred
regard to his laws, may not ftill, in a political capacity,
be entitled to great merit; and be a proper perfon to be
concerned in guiding the helm of ftate. Long experience in civil affairs, it is faid—a fuperior knowledge of
the laws—a facility of fpeaking and of difpatching bufi-
nefs—the difcovery of arts ufeful to government, are
qualifications neceffary to promote the good of the
ftate, which is the main end of all government. a hon

Perhaps we may allow of the exception, provided
there is nothing in the perfonal character of fuch, from
which the ftate may apprehend greater danger, or in-
convenience, than it can expect good, from their capacity to ferve it.

Still it holds good, that men of probity,—of virtue,—of religion ought, in all well regulated ftates, to
be the objects of the people's choice, both from the
natural tendency of virtue to promote the happinefs
of a nation, and from the influence of a good example; which has, in perfons diftinguifhed by the confidence of their brethren, a fenfible and powerful influence towards rendering religion and virtue more
generally efteemed, and practifed. This confideration
will have the greater weight, if we reflect, that (as we
have fhewn) moft of the flourifhing ftates in the
world, have owed their origin and increafe to virtue
and righteoufnefs; fo, as the manners of the people
grew more diffolute and corrupt, they gradually declined in power, in wealth, in credit.

It

IT would be going out of my proper fphére, and perhaps invading the province of the Chief Magiftrate, to enter into a detail of thofe objects, which claim the attention of the General Court, in their prefent or future feffions, in the courfe of this year. Their own good fenfe, their political knowledge, and their perfect acquaintance with the internal ftate of the Commonwealth, will point out, and lead them to adopt fuch meafures, as prefent exigencies require.

OUR civil fathers, however, will permit me to remind them, that it is righteoufnefs only which exalteth a nation; that it can never be good policy to tranfgrefs the facred rules of juftice and fidelity; and, that the grand fecret of political wifdom is to maintain a fteady and untainted integrity. They will, therefore, for the fupport of publick faith and honour, as well as domeftick tranquillity, pay the ftricteft attention to commutative juftice and equity, by a faithful obfervance and fulfilment of all publick engagements; remembering that publick contracts are as binding, as private ones can be fuppofed to be; and ought to be difcharged with the fame good faith and punctuality; and that no nation can make the leaft pretenfion to the character of a righteous one, that does not pay a facred regard to its promifes and contracts.

THEY will maintain inviolate, by a ftrict adherence to its original principles, our happy conftitution of government; and, for the purpofes of national happinefs and glory, they will fupport and ftrengthen the federal government of the United States, by every
conftitutional

constitutional means in their power ; fully perſuaded that the continuance of our national government is eſſential to our independence, our ſafety, our very exiſtence as an empire.

Our civil rulers, will think themſelves obliged, both in their publick and private ſtations, to propagate a ſpirit of induſtry, frugality, and ſobriety, among all ranks of people ; to encourage agriculture, commerce and arts ; and, to promote the intereſts of literature and ſcience ; from the ſtrongeſt conviction, that ignorance and liberty are incompatible ; that the former is the parent of deſpotiſm, and the nurſe of ſuperſtition. In fine, they will do all in their power, that wiſdom and knowledge may be the ſtability of our times—that all vice and impiety be ſuppreſſed, and that the people may be allured to the practice of that righteouſneſs, which exalteth a nation. In order to this, they will ſhew, in their own perſons, that they are not aſhamed of the goſpel of Chriſt, by paying all due regard to his ſacred inſtitutions, and obedience to his laws.

Sensible of the difficulties of their taſk, and of their need of divine aid and ſupport, we commend them to him, who giveth wiſdom to the wiſe, and underſtanding to the prudent ; beſeeching him to direct and proſper all their conſultations, to the advancement of his glory, the good of his church, the ſafety, honour and welfare of the people of this Commonwealth, and of United America.

F   Permit

PERMIT me to conclude, by reminding this whole assembly, that it concerns every one to live in the practice of religion and virtue; not only as the publick prosperity is deeply concerned in it, but as their own personal happiness, both here and hereafter, absolutely depends upon it. Godliness is profitable for all things, having the promise of this life, and of that which is to come. As therefore we wish the prosperity of our country; as we wish to enjoy the comforts of the present world; as we are anxious to meet the approbation of God, and to enjoy his favour in Heaven; let us become the sincere disciples of JESUS CHRIST; let us follow peace with all men, and holiness, without which no man shall see the Lord. Let the recollection, that the eyes of GOD are against those who do evil, and of that indignation, which he will finally pour upon the ungodly, deter us from all iniquity, and lead us to aspire after that genuine piety, which will most assuredly, through the infinite merits and mediation of JESUS CHRIST, introduce us to the future vision and fruition of GOD, where we shall see him as he is, and know even as we are known.

www.ingramcontent.com/pod-product-compliance
Lightning Source LLC
Chambersburg PA
CBHW021600270326
41931CB00009B/1306